teach me about

Pets

Copyright © Joy Berry, 2022
Originally Published, 1986

All rights are reserved.

No part of this book can be duplicated or used without the prior written permission of the copyright owner, except for the use of brief quotations from the book.

For inquiries or permission requests contact the publisher.

Published by Joy Berry Enterprises
www.joyberryenterprises.com

teach me about

By JOY BERRY

Illustrated by Bartholomew

A pet is an animal who lives with people. There are many different kinds of pets.

Pets need food.

They need to be fed

their own special food

every day.

Pets need water.

They need to have fresh water every day.

Pets need special places

in which to stay.

These places need

to be kept clean.

Pets need to move around.

They need space

in which they can move.

Pets need to rest and sleep.

Some pets need to be taught

how to be good pets.

They need to learn

what they should do.

They need to learn

what they should not do.

Pets need extra care when they are hurt or sick. Sometimes they need to be taken to a doctor. Doctors for animals are called veterinarians. They help take care of pets who are hurt or sick. They also do things to keep pets from getting sick.

Pets need someone to pay attention to them. They need someone to talk to them and play with them. Most pets need someone to touch them in a kind, loving way.

When pets get the things they need, they are happy. Pets that are happy are good pets. They do what they are supposed to do. They do things that make the people around them feel good.

Pets are unhappy when they do not get the things they need. Pets who are unhappy often do what they are not supposed to do. Sometimes they do things that upset the people around them.

Pets do not like to be treated badly.
They do not like to be hit,
kicked, pinched, or squeezed.
They do not like people to pull
on their fur, ears, or tails.
Pets do not like to be picked
up or touched all the time.
Sometimes pets like to be
left alone.

Sometimes pets get frightened when people treat them badly.

Sometimes they show their fear by trying to hurt the people who are hurting them. Sometimes they bite, scratch, or kick.

Many pets are afraid of people they do not know.

They are afraid that the people might hurt them.

Some pets act differently around people they do not know.

Sometimes they bite, scratch, kick, or hiss.

Other times they growl, whine, hide, or run away.

You should stay away

from pets you do not know

so they do not hurt you.

If you do not want pets to hurt you, you must not treat them badly.

You must also give them the things they need.

helpful hints for parents about

Dear Parents:

The purpose of this book is
- to develop in children an attitude of respect and responsibility in regard to pets, and
- to teach children appropriate ways to treat pets.

You can best implement the purpose of this book by
- reading it to your child, and
- reading the following *Helpful Hints* and using them whenever applicable.

CONSIDERING A PET

When considering a pet for your child, you may want to examine the potential benefits that pets can provide children. The special relationship that a child and pet establish can enhance a child's development in the following ways:

- A pet teaches a child responsibility for other living creatures.
- A pet helps a child learn to be gentle, humane, and respectful of all other forms of life.
- A pet can help a child understand the reproductive process and the life and death cycles.
- A pet offers constant love and companionship without being judgmental, asking questions, or reprimanding.

Parent's responsibility

As the parent, you will have the ultimate responsibility for the care of your child's pet. This is an important aspect of pet ownership which you need to consider. Before deciding on a pet for your child, ask yourself the following questions:

- Will you take the time to ensure the pet receives proper care, which may include feeding, exercising, cleaning cages, and housebreaking a puppy?
- Do you have the patience and knowledge to teach your child responsible pet ownership?
- Did you enjoy pets as a child, and do you enjoy animals?

It is necessary for parents to show an interest in the pet and share in its care and training. A child needs to learn that it is a privilege to own a pet, and he or she must earn the rewards of ownership through responsible care. The parent with a positive relationship to the pet is also an important role model for the child.

Environmental considerations

Before choosing a pet for children, parents should evaluate their environment and lifestyle. You may want to consider:

- your family—What are the ages and interests of your children?
- your schedule—Is there someone at home all day?
- space—How much protected space do you have available for a pet?

- cost—Can you afford the pet and its maintenance?
- health considerations—Does anyone in the family have allergies or phobias?
- other restrictions—Are there rental laws or local ordinances which limit pet ownership?

SELECTING A PET

When you have evaluated your family's lifestyle, environment, and interests, you are ready to select a pet. It is important to match the pet to the needs, capabilities, and temperament of the child recipient. Don't give a child more than he or she can handle. Since you as the parent are ultimately responsible, be sure you are capable of assuming some of the duties. Remember, a pet is not disposable. The responsibility that you and your family assume continues for the life of the pet.

Some popular pet choices for children

Some pets are more suitable for young children than others. Parents will need to decide if the child is capable of caring for the pet properly. The following are some of the more common pets you might wish to consider:

- *Dogs* are excellent, responsive pets but often shed and require exercise, space, and regular veterinary treatment. Puppies require a lot of attention and cleanup which a small child cannot provide. However, a puppy is a good pet for a child to grow with because it is an affectionate playmate which is able to give and receive love. An older dog that has been raised with children is also a good choice if you wish to avoid housebreaking and training. Remember, a small child (three to seven years) cannot properly bathe, train, or exercise a dog, so these duties become the parents' responsibility.
- *Cats* require less space and are easier to housebreak, but they also shed and require litter box maintenance. Cats are often less responsive to small children than dogs, and they tend to bite and scratch more readily.
- *Birds* such as parakeets and cockatiels are intelligent and lively but may bite small fingers, and the cage maintenance is difficult for small children. Songbirds are usually less responsive, and children may lose interest quickly.
- *Fish* are interesting to look at and an inexpensive investment, but provide

no physical contact. Children often kill fish by overfeeding, and cleaning the tank is a parental responsibility.
- *Rabbits* make good pets for small children because they are intelligent, easy to keep, and can be housebroken or kept outdoors. However, rabbits can kick, scratch, and have special habits to consider such as chewing and digging.
- *Guinea pigs, rats,* and *gerbils* are laboratory animals which make excellent first pets for children from age three to seven. Hamsters also make good pets, but are nocturnal and tend to bite more easily. All these small animals can provide valuable lessons in basic pet care, and with a little practice can be handled by most young children.
- *Small amphibians, reptiles,* and even *insects* can also be kept easily in terrariums on a shelf. Although they don't require much care, they have special food and temperature requirements.

Exotic or wild animals seldom make good pets because they are difficult to care for, are more susceptible to rabies, and never really become tame. Wild animals are better left in their natural environment or in zoos where they can receive proper care.

The first pet

If you have never had a pet, try to visit friends to see how they live with their pets. During the visit you can
- watch and play with the pet,
- ask about the cost and care of the pet, and
- offer to pet-sit or care for a friend's pet for a few days in your home.

Allergies

Borrowing pets can determine if anyone in your family has allergies to certain animals. Sometimes an allergy appears only after prolonged contact with an animal. If there is a history of allergies in your family, your child should be tested before you acquire a new pet. You may want to consult your doctor or veterinarian about an allergy-free pet.

Phobias

Some children suffer from an unwarranted fear of animals. You can help your child overcome these fears by following these guidelines:

- Remove your child from threatening situations.
- Don't negate your child's fear by telling him or her it's silly to be afraid, and don't allow others to ridicule your child.
- Reassure your child calmly that the animals will not hurt him or her.
- Encourage your child to observe others playing with or grooming animals.
- Visit zoos or circuses to see animals at a safe distance.

However, parents should instill in their children a healthy fear of strange or wild animals which they should avoid.

BRINGING THE PET HOME

After your family has decided on a pet and you have discussed the responsibilities of ownership with your child, you are ready to bring the pet home. Be sure that you have done the following:
- acquired the necessary food and supplies;
- involved your child in the preparations so that he or she is aware of what the new pet needs;
- determined the space your pet will occupy, including feeding areas;
- acquired the name of a veterinarian for future reference;
- decided on the feeding schedule and responsibilities; and
- chosen a name for a puppy or kitten so it can begin to respond.

After the new pet has arrived, the parent must act as a role model by providing guidance in proper handling and care. The child and the pet require supervision. Small children can unconsciously injure pets and must be taught proper ways to stroke, lift, and hold them. It is important to protect both the child and the pet. A small puppy or kitten may bite or scratch when handled improperly. Because of the time and effort required to prepare for a new pet, it is not wise to give pets as surprise gifts. If you want to make a gift of a pet, you should discuss the matter with the prospective family and be sure that they are eager and prepared to accept the responsibility.

INTRODUCING YOUR PET TO A NEW BABY

If you plan to bring a new baby into your home and you already have a pet, there are several preparatory steps you should follow:

- Have your veterinarian check your pet's health.
- Have the house fumigated to control fleas.
- Don't reject your pet or disrupt its schedule as you prepare for the new baby.
- Allow the pet into the nursery to sniff around.

When the new baby comes home, continue to be conscious of your pet's relationship to the newcomer.

- Introduce your pet to the new baby by holding the baby and allowing the pet to sniff the baby all over.
- Take the time to provide a little extra attention for your pet to prevent rivalry.
- Never leave the pet alone with the baby. Use a gate for the nursery and put a net over the crib.
- Protect the pet later on from a toddler's pestering by setting aside an area where the pet can eat and rest peacefully.

GIVING UP A PET

How to find a home

Sometimes families discover that they cannot keep a pet because of unforeseen changes in lifestyle or environment. If you find yourself in this situation, it is critical that your child understands the reasons for giving up the pet. Always emphasize the welfare and happiness of the animal as the ultimate reason for your decision. You can help alleviate some of the distress by asking your child to help you find a home for your pet. You can do this by

- placing an ad in the local newspaper or on radio,
- putting notices on neighborhood bulletin boards or at work, asking your friends and co-workers,
- calling the Humane Society about the possibility of someone adopting your pet, and
- consulting your veterinarian for a referral.

Never just abandon your animal or drop him or her off at the pound to be destroyed. If you find that it is impossible to find a suitable home for your pet, it is better to have him painlessly put to sleep by your veterinarian.

PET DISEASES

Catching diseases from pets

Parents, as prospective pet owners, may justifiably wonder about the possibility of catching a disease from a pet. Although it is possible to catch certain diseases, it is much less likely than catching a disease from another human. In fact, the risk of contracting a disease from a pet is so small that it is practically nil. There are a few simple precautions that you can take to further reduce the chances of catching a disease from your pet.

- Vaccinate your pet for common diseases such as rabies and distemper, and leukemia in cats.
- Don't allow your pet to wander loose where it may come in contact with sick or wild animals.
- Always wash your hands after playing with or handling your pet.
- Control fleas and ticks on your dog or cat and in your house and yard.
- Avoid direct contact with animal feces, especially by toddlers.
- Avoid cleaning the cat litter box if you are pregnant. Cat feces can harbor the cause of illness called toxoplasmosis which is potentially threatening to both mother and fetus.
- Keep cats and other animals out of play yard sandboxes.

Sick animals should receive immediate professional attention from a veterinarian who can identify and treat the illness while alleviating any fears of contagion to humans.

WHEN A PET ISN'T POSSIBLE

When time, space, or health considerations prevent you from having a pet, there are alternatives which will give your child the benefits of a relationship with animals. Your child can

- participate in organizations such as 4-H Club and Junior Humane Societies where a child can take part without ownership;
- sponsor a pet at the zoo or museum;
- offer to pet-sit for friends;
- maintain a wild bird feeder; or
- observe animals in nature at local parks.

www.ingramcontent.com/pod-product-compliance
Lightning Source LLC
Chambersburg PA
CBHW081409070526
44583CB00020B/2746